A Philosophy of Yard

Jack Kolkmeyer

Delray Beach, Florida
2017

Forte Publishing

First Published in 2017
Published by:

FORTE Publications
#12 Ashmun Street
Snapper Hill
Monrovia, Liberia
[+231] 88-110-6177
[+231] 777-155-923

FORTE Publishing
7202 Tavenner Lane
208 Alexandria
VA, 22306

FORTE Press
76 Sarasit Road
Ban Pong, 70110
Ratchaburi, Thailand
[+66] 85-824-4382

http://fortepublishing.wix.com/fppp
fortepublishing@gmail.com

ISBN-10: 0994534795
ISBN-13: 978-0994534798

Dedication

This collection is dedicated to my partner,

Jinny Ritter,

for providing me the time and space to write; to my loving

and sweet little family, and to the tribe of creative individuals

who have always supported my adventurous writing impulses.

Thanks, also, to FORTE Publishing for the continuing collaboration.

Introduction

A Philosophy of Yard

The great places of the world are reflections of the past, the present and the future. They also reflect how differently individuals and groups perceive them. But, so are the intimate and minute moments that we pass in our own small, personal environments.

To me the work that I have done as a city planner and writer and the way I have perceived that work, has always, in part, been related to my fondness for and gratitude to, **The Imagist Poets:** T.E. Hulme, Wallace Stevens, William Carlos Williams, Ezra Pound, Amy Lowell, D.H Lawrence...all of them. Their idea that any given moment or any viewed object or place will be interpreted differently by anyone who regards it, is a unique metaphor for "place". Everyone enjoys a transformative and magic experience in evocative places, as they are, indeed, poetic moments. That poetry, for me, begins in my own back yard.

The Romantic Poets, especially Keats, Shelley and Byron have clearly influenced my desire to write about unique settings and exotic places and **The Beat Poets**, Kerouac, Ferlinghetti, Di Prima and Ginsberg, in particular, taught me about the different ways to understand meter and flow. And finally, a special cadre of African and African-American poets, Leopold Senghor, Wole Soyinka, Maya Angelou and Langston Hughes instilled in me the need to write with soulfulness.

But most of all, to the incredible places around the world that have inspired all of this writing. Some are large and elegant, others small and off the beaten path, some of which include: Cincinnati, Peebles and Athens Ohio; Pittsburgh, PA; Delray Beach and St. Petersburg, FL. Then, there are others like Paris, France; Santa Fe and Taos, NM; Amsterdam, The Netherlands; Kpaiyea, Liberia; Boston, MA; Nassau, Bahamas; Chicago, IL; San Diego, Los Angeles, San Simeon and Cambria, CA; San Antonio, TX; Salamanca, Spain; Lisbon, Alfama, Coimbra and Porto, Portugal; Neuchatel and Colombier, Switzerland; Bloomington, IN; and Burlington, CO and many more.

The pieces in this book include both poems and songs. They span a period from the 1960's to the present.

The Corn Dancers has previously appeared in **The Writers Place.**

The Faces of Elder Wisdom and several other poems were initially published in **KWEE: Liberian Literary Magazine.**

Table of Contents

often as a child

I perched on the quilted corner
of the old oaken bed
my grandfather died in

warm inside a house prepared for winter

watching
my grandmother and her head

sitting in the dim protracted light
of her tarnished bureau mirror

brushing
ecstatic fireflies from her hair

Cincinnati

A Philosophy of Yard

there is a philosophy
blooming in this yard
      among the stones and plants
      and seeds and weeds
that call this terrain their home

there is a sense of place
that changes with the weather
      and the seasons
      and the animal ways

there is a friendship here
      a bond of sorts
with the sun and the wind and the rain
      the insect fights
      the turnings of the worms
      and the bird flights

the watchfulness of all who come here
      to play to eat or to retreat
      hoping to avoid
      the stress of some conflicting times
that bring the desiccation and the heat

and there are the stones
standing sentinel among the pathways
    providing respite
    in their shades
and water in their cracks

everything can grow and rearrange
with time and space
    and the care to cultivate a fertile mind
    willing to help along
    the systems that weave
    themselves so tightly in this place
and along these tracks

there is a philosophy
blooming in this yard

Delray Beach

Autumn

fall arrived early this year
      not that it sometimes does not
but once again the season changed
      no pealing of the church chimes
      not a hint of myrrhing aroma
      nor a scent of fragrant frankincense
to mark such a lofty engagement

just another day
another shifting from summer to fall
      more a day of sad farewell to that last lusty embrace
of summer's warmth
      and all of the fun in the sun that was had by all

and now we just wait with resignation knowing that winter
is near
      as we prepare a warmer spot
      amidst the moves and rearrangements

not that we really care
about the seasons and the times

we know they reoccur
but it is always the fall that colors its way in
        with a different and alluring sense
in the annual scope of changes

except for those who live with the soil
        and extract their faith from dirt
        and sweat and toil
        for those who work without a shirt
they know it's time to take stock

just another day
another shifting from summer to fall
        more a day of sad farewell to summer
        and all of the fun that was had by all

just another season
in the cycle that circles on

and on

Delray Beach

the pod people

we are the pod people
gravid with the presence of another era
full of spawn from other astral places
      that we still cannot imagine
      or have not yet even seen in our dreams

      but we are in deed
      the seed people
      planting ourselves along the furrows of time
      seen differently from star to star
      but passing ever so quickly
      from the then to the now
pointing once again
to the infinity reach
      the never ending reality of truth

and the messages
     that the stars teach

     we are the plant people
     germinated with the love of the sun
     and the affection of rain
     gametes from other deeply seeded choices
     now rooted in the ground
     where all roots are grounded
in their function
and their purpose

as we sustain

watching the starts

with our feet in the dirt

Delray Beach

Musée d'Orsay

I want to dive into an impressionist painting
and splash my way through
the burnished blues and greens
and muted mauves

I'll surround myself with shifting colors
in the hope they blend me into serenity

I'm going to leave my disconnected shapes
and dive into an impressionist
painting

get stuck in the moment
      of a Monet sunrise
whirl away with wispy
      Degas dancers
get lost in a verdant
      Gaugin jungle

become a woman
ironing by the sea
with a view
brush the sunshine
with short sisterly strokes

while having lunch
on the grass
at no cost

I'm going to dive into
an impressionist painting
and fall asleep
for awhile

on a lily pad

Paris

Walking Up the Down Road

we met for the first time
    at the confluence of two chances
    one went this way and the other went that way there
we walked along the destinies of our choices
theirs went through the forest of thought
mine along the valleys of work

we met a second time
so far down our paths
    somewhere upstream
    between the rivers of our decisions
theirs contemplative and quiet
mine more riotous and boisterous

and now we meet again
here at the estuary of life
    having meandered up
    and back down again
through all the indecisions
    of hope and dreams
    and opportunities made splendid

then gone away

we shook hands
then hugged
then sat and talked for a while
     about where we had been
     and what we had seen
     and what we had tried

we smiled and laughed
but then grew still
     as we watched the waters
     of one way
converge with the expanse of another

back at the start again
of our two chances

Delray Beach

The Corn Dancers

you always wait patiently
for that flicker of light green
to break on through
to the upper side
from the seed
planted with a prayer
to your grandmother
who showed you how
to stick your finger in the ground
and gently plant the maize force
pointy side down

you wait longingly
for that one-time morning
when you a seedling watcher
a cloud enshrouded dawn talker
mark these mornings on the horizon
along the mountain moorings
so next year you know again
the precise relationship
between your plantings
and the solar almanac
as the seeds become sun spurts
a reminder that springs have not changed
for millennia gone before

you visually anticipate
the color blind mutations
the herbal maturation
from slender stalking youth
to the laying forth of leaves
that quickly learn
their rhythmic rustling
musical patterns
played in soft duets
with Aeolian companions
while rooted harmonically
in the ground

you pace repeatedly
on your well-worn
garden stones
you water and you pry
you prod the soil
you poke around

watching for invaders
from the air
or underground

you celebrate
that youthful graduation
as tessellation heralds change
from growth to obligation
springing forth the need
to propagate
and the relentless urge
of promulgation
beautifully embellished
on the serpent's skin
hiding crumbled
in your garden
of the eaten

you know the feel
of those silky golden strands
on their first moist moments
and you stroke them as your lover
but you can only watch
the mad male pollen
pulsed by summer sirens
into the fertile covens
of the sultry afternoon

you hear with their ears
     the blissful falling of days
     the insect songs of night
     the wistful bird flights
     the patient rabbit heartbeats

and you finally see
a kernel of
     past oral truth
peering from its
     husky linen coat
and you know the wait is over
as the amber waves hello

a somber harvest moon
reigns remindingly
in the obsidian night sky

and for a moment

     you are saddened
that these
     once a year life spans
have fled
     so fleetingly
     so relentlessly
with such growing abandon

and then you hear the
        ancient
        corn
        dancers
the scratching of their
        sun
        bleached
        bones
the dancing of their
        drying
        dying
        endosperms
the rattle of their
        rustic
        rhythmic
        rhythms
playing softer duets
still rooted harmonically
in the ground you kneel respectfully
in admiration toward the sound
and then you see the
        ancient
        corn
        dancers
as winter steps along

Santa Fe

Take Me to Your Edge

Take me to your edge
to the precipice of your time
      your past, your present and your future
to the misty cliff of your knowing
from which we can leap
      behind the clouds
into the unknowing moments
we now share

Take me to the edge
of your soul
to sit and remember
with your friends and lovers
      who you are
      where you've been
to see the longing in your heart
the short cuts
through the maze
of actions and adventures
past the forks in the road
leaving them all behind

for me

Take me to the edge
of your spirit
dangle me over your mirth
      and warmth and affection
tease me with your life

and your momentum
touch me with your grace
        and your charm
alarm me with your might

and your might not

Take me to the edge
        of your body
        to the inner workings of your heart
        to that moment
        when your emotions
stand taut with the anticipation
        of our touch
take me to your inner taste
wrap your arms around my waist

Take me to the edge
        of your love
take me there now
to that vast expanse
        into which we've only just stepped
        take me there now
        and whisper to me

all the secrets that you've kept
all this time
singing all those melodies and rhymes

from deep in your heart

Take me to the edge
of your life
take me there now
take me to your edge
so that I can see
       the center of your love
       the center of you
       the center of your essence
       the center of the circle
of the axis of who we are

and where we've been
and the pledge we've kept

Take me to your edge

Santa Fe

Seek a Higher Vantage Point

when scouting a new direction

seek a higher vantage point
with a peripheral grasp of
both hills and pebbles
to view the context
of your intention

when searching for another path
among the trees of respite and can't
through the mires of discontent
find a new meander to the summit
for a vision that converts
an elephant to an ant

when wanting a new angle
from which to measure the arc
of resistance to your habits
and to free you from the old ways

to hunt and gather
fierce new freedoms
with the heart of rebel

seek a higher vantage point

Santa Fe

Pacing

pacing around these lessons
very curious as to their intentions

ignoring certain appearances
      as the heart beats bleat
      their blood bent notes
around so many inclinations

racing around the lesions
      on my body mind
curious as to their infections
while the nerve tufts tinge
      my many colored coats
as a means of protection

pissing around allegiance
curious as to the meaning of alliance
while ignoring the ego panes
      frosted from the cold notions
that surround my allegiance

to what

the peering inside
no longer
seems old and remote

Santa Fe

The Primitive

take me back to the primitive
one stone at a time
root by root
myth by myth

take me back to the primal mist
to a time of fire and rocks and water
to the birth of hot
and strength and clarity

teach me to enkindle
and speak like a bird
and sit still for an era
like a boulder

throw me to the wolves
of hunt and gather
as I search and scratch
for my needs and desires

lift me up to the superlative
to the rhyme of a mother tongue
for the love a father land
to the hope of a prodigal son and
to the need for an honorable daughter

to the death of everything
I forgot

teach me to rekindle
the warmth of an old word
and to listen to a culture
that I shoulder

and to act and be blunt
about heart and soul fires

I want to go forward to
a new past time
of flesh and bone
of frankincense and myrrh

I want to get down on my knees
to mud
and mortality
and dirt

take me back to the primitive
to the naked ember of fire
to aspire
to get down

back to the fire
to the stone
to the root

take me back to the time
of the tone age of listening
back to the lithic stories
sculpted in mythic art

take me back there
to the primal verge

one stone at a time

root by root

myth by myth

Santa Clara Pueblo

Dig My Roots (a song)

Give me little wisdom
Every now and then
It ain't very often
But even then

Picture someone
With a good sense of sound
Try to keep your situation
On the ground

Home...home...home
That's where I want to go
Please send me home

Show me my culture
Dig my roots
Show me my culture
And dig my roots

Give me little pleasure
Every now and then
But give me security
In the end

Picture your mother
with a good sense of sound
Try to keep your situation
On the ground

Home...home...home
That's where I want to go
Please send me home

Show me my culture
Dig my roots
Show me my culture
And dig my roots
Walk me through the garden
Of earthly delights
Give me back my land
And respect my rights

Picture your parents
When they're not around
Try to keep your situation
On the ground

Home...home...home
That's where I want to go
Please send me home

Show me my culture
Dig my roots
Show me my culture
And dig my roots

Show me what my grandma did
Way back then

It ain't very often
But even then

Picture yourself
Bein' lost and then found
Try to keep your situation
On the ground

Home...home...home
That's where I want to go
Please send me home

Show me my culture
Dig my roots
Show me my culture
And dig my roots

Santa Fe

π

when *pi* are squared
      a message bears its bones
      in numbers telling secrets
of a juncture down the road

when *pi* is bared
      a codex clears its throat
      in numbers telling times
on reams of ancient rhymes

papers withered and minds forgot
      but numbers better fared
as answers sit unfold there neatly
as answers unfurl there neatly
when *pi* are squared πr^2

a circumference halved by diameter
      unlocks a lost refrain
      a distinctly embossed pentameter
on a very old terrain

numbers never lie
      though they lay there numbly
crafted in the stones
that angles left behind

papers withered and minds forgot
      but numbers better spared
the answers that rest there clearly
when *pi* are squared

The Mound Builders

centuries of ozymandian thoughts
and eons of gordian knots
begin to untangle
watching the hilly serpent
slither motionless in the grass
      through the seeping veins of southern Ohio

seeing is believing and hearing divine
wondering where the wander went
      around these lush hills
themselves like bodies sleeping
      in their night beds mounds of soil
now a very long time ago
some say
a whole lot of worlds
just slipped away

all kinds of people
speaking a rapture of words
the whole ancient planet
has gone to the birds

remnants of previous times
are old manifestations
trapped inside these tribal effigies
winging off in time travel flights
      journeys without maps
to the ebb and flow of eons

time traveling is the best
.

there is a mental doorway
that opens into another era
        another place
        another revelation
a passage that no one showed you
until now

there's a unique solipsistic web
hanging over these hills
there's a twist in the line of time
there is a reason and a rhyme

the past radiates a message
that enlivens the now

the planet has shifted
we've gone for a cruise
the planet has gifted
a chosen few

consider that dinosaurs
walked with men
that both creation and evolution
have been infinity sent

to think that these gentle
terrestrial mounds
are amphoric remembrances
bubbling up over layers of mournings
here an uncle there a son
there an aunt here a daughter
the decision to rest on the earth
rather than in it
implies another kind of wishful thinking
another stroke of wistful aspiring

a lump of ancestors
plowed under the influence
of newcomers
and their amber graves of wane
their amber waves of grain

just a pile of old bones
making way for a new terrain

level the barbarian hillocks
full of trinkets thrown around
they were primitives
maybe even savage
time to rearrange
to our altered meandering dimensions

how long does it take
to stack up a generation
or two or three
how long to tear it down

discoveries are accidents
history is incidence
bound by momentary glimpses
of passing shadows
momentary reelings
transient waves of lost coincidence

for now
just motionless in the grass
in southern Ohio

short cadenzas and a maddening twirls
little furrows of patterned gravitations
time is bleached by the sun
drying mournfully in the wind

staring at a grassy protruding sepulcher
the day swirls around
like an angry leaf
not quite ready to fall

sitting alone now
by my father's own fresh mound
not too far removed
from the serpent's mound
rewinding our lives
wishing it had been some other way
a tad more time
a procession
of our extended family members
appears from the murky mysteries
of the woodlands
bearing baskets of fresh cut flowers
these are the hours of us
we built the mountains of love

Enki did it
Buddha did it
Jesus did it
and so did Mohammed

we are the mound builders of now

The Great Serpent Mound Peebles, Ohio

33

Running Around in Circles

there was a time
before the current bird speak
and plant philosophies
when geometry of the stars
prevailed

there was a time
when circles cast their lots
in over stones
holdings stellar secrets in their midst
for all to see
at home on the ground
or on a journey in the sky ways

there was an inner connected time
of pyramids and hexagons
and octagons and pentangles
and mysteries held in *pi*
when angels sang their rhymes
and languages
first took a peek
and we could plant our seeds
under foot

there was a time
a moment gone by
      for now
but soon to be unveiled
so once again
we can know the roots

and
      all run around
in circles

all over again

as time goes by

Summer Solstice
Delray Beach

The Other Side

sitting here
looking over there
      wondering
how is it
      that they live that way
      surrounded by the things
      that so closely embrace them
astounded by the light and dark
      that seems to always so tightly
shelter them
impounded in a style that
      is truly only theirs

why do they sing their songs that way
      mostly at night but sometimes at dawn
and speak the way they do to each other
      in tongues full of rhythm and rhyme

there must be a reason why
they gather about in circles
      holdings hands
and spend so much time and energy
      doing things on their lands

why do they only walk
        when they come this way
and never drive a car
and always insist on smiling
        and asking how you are

so grounded in a smile that
is truly only theirs

sitting here
looking over there
        wondering
if there is a way
to visit
        over there
        sometime
in the future
        on the other side

Delray Beach

Triste Tropique

One can hardly comprehend Africa
      in a thought
let alone in a mythic river or two
or in a splattering enjunglement
      of legend and lore
or in olympic mountains where simians play
      across stretches of beast inflected savannahs
or in old davidic gorges
      where bones sit as storytellers
or in all the human beings that were bought and sold

one can hardly imagine Africa
      in a dance
let alone in stilt walking prancers
      or dervishes whirling in a raffia ruse
      of roots gone down deep before
or in masks that smile and talk in tongues
or in drums that beat in linguistic meter
      with rattles that shake in blood beat tones
or in all the spirits that drift in and out
      of human trance

one can hardly conjure Africa
     in a scheme
let alone in tribal tribulations
or in god forsaken fever ridden wanderings
     of journeys without maps
or in philosophies animistic in their nature
or in curings medicinal in their charms

or in desires to be left alone
because of the fear of strangers
     and strange forebodings

in a full moon dream
     of diamonds and gold

one can hardly comprehend Africa

Kpaiyea, Liberia

a peninsula in summer

standing at the end of the peninsula
as the sun peeks a solar eye
        across the horizon
on the first rays of summer

you see things
and hear them
        in a different melody
from that place that brought you here

today's peninsula of thinking
was long ago an island of another mind
        connected by an isthmus of imagination
colored by those times

looking east
staring directly into the eyes
        of the glaring simmering beast
        on the solstice rising on a glimmer thread
        dangling
        between the living and the dead
        from a small flat topped promontory
        of igneous bearing stone
you feel things in a different light

watching one another
building fires of intention
hunting fishing singing and wishing

you hope now only to aspire

discontinuing the connections
        to make an obsidian point
        absorbing the energies of this estranged place
you have faith in the spark to kindle the flames
        of togetherness and aspiration
even as the faith in our times
        seems again to be sinking

into the sands of another deep dimension

Key West

streaming

sitting by the creek
watching tadpoles and water snakes
     define the limits of their lives
as ripples jump and sway
a water bug runs away
     from a frog's tongue licking
and there really lurks a mire down there

when you are young
you are certain beyond the shadow of a gnat
     that some dreadful heinous ogre
     skulks in the very pleasure of that creamy mud
you know that for a fact

as strapping and fetching teenage people
we loved this meander
     because of love and drinking
     and laughter and youth
     and because we could wretch here
     in the safety of our lilting stream
you know that for a fact

so today I sidled on over
        to where I thought the little rivulet
        snaked its earlier path
and it wasn't there

no tadpoles no frogs no snakes
this is now where people park their cars
my heart dropped to the hot asphalt
        but the thought of watching a stick or a leaf
        that you could prod along
        float down this creek
        until it too just disappeared
        or you lost sight of it
        as your own meander took its turns
still sticks in the front of your mind
you know that for a fact

because you can recall the times and the faces
you can remember
sitting by the creek

Cincinnati

why seagulls can't fish

a sudden blurry of fish
agitates the clear blue calm
a whirlpool of fin and flash
jumping and skipping
to a mad piscine polka

and then the gulls
descend
harpies
squawking and wailing
hungry for their link
in the food chain
aviatic bomber pilots
raiding down
on the frantic fish parade

they dive
they peck
they slap
on a mission for what is theirs

they swirl around
they prey
intoxicated by a bubbling
aquadisiac

but
for some aqueous reason
perhaps a seasonal secret
or a still unexplained
neptunian trap

they catch no fish
skewer no gill
pierce no fin
impale not one armorous scale

though they have their chance
so
     it must be an ancient fish and bird
dance

Nassau, Bahamas

The Infinity Thing
Musings at The Dali Museum

it's hard to grasp
the infinity thing

the appearance and disappearance
of time into helic rings

that elastic melting and morphing
sliding away from faces we clasp
close to our breast

with such adherence to rhyme

constantly pelting
         the best of our intentions
         and the reality of our dreams
with dripping shadows of the long legs
         of our daddies
and the back sides of our maiden voyages
into the enigma
of eternity disguised as infinity

it's hard to grasp
the infinity thing

St. Petersburg, Florida

Time is Linen

undoing
a moment past

a swerve along a time line

time is linen
flapping on the line

still going
an ocean passed
a verb among renowns
love is a raven
soaring on the skyline

belonging

a song that lasts
with notes along a rhyme line
sound is a siren
tugging on the mind

undoing a moment past
time is linen flapping on the line
one end flaps in
the other comes out

Santa Fe

A Tuscan Afternoon

a Tuscan afternoon
overlooking
the fading rusty bloodlets
of the brooding
Sangre de Cristo
foothills

a Jurassic blast of O'Keefe
wafts over
an aged bronzed attitude
on a winter's edge
nudged along by the unsympathetic
soulfulness of sunlight
come late

as you feel
a Tuscan red afternoon
ironic in a sense
melding somnolent cultures
into oxidic twists
of
ironic fate

a Tuscan afternoon
overlooking
the odd ancientness
and the old eccentricity
of
Santa Fe

keeping faith
and
paying the bills
on
a Tuscan afternoon

watching the hills

Santa Fe

Irises

the irises have converged
again in the garden

the floral monks
coming from the east
with the glorious rising sun
have gathered
with their yellow beards
and majestic mitres
to flower their annual messages
on the terrestrial faithful

once more

they parade passionately
in bright solar vestments
bishops all
making their solemn moves

the irises have massed

the flop eared friars
have arrived in royalty

bearing pragmatic standards
and vernal messages

whispering wind words
from legendary focus

the irises are here

ora pra nobis
pray for us

Santa Fe

At the Van Gogh Museum
Amsterdam

The Chairs of Van Gogh and Gaugin (1888)

my friend is a chair

somber and alone
on the ochre notions
of his straw seat

simple but accidentally eclectic
roaming from chromate
glimpses
in to blue other tones

the disparate nature
of his own recollected
visions
become muted
in this solitary seat

somewhere
outside
a cottage at nightfall

on a swirling
starry night

on any given day
my friend is a chair

Animistic Encounters

we stared at each other
for a protracted moment
and then she tired of me

and retracted
back into the bushes

Athens, Ohio

an ant
is a proverbial titan
I considered

crushing it
between my fingers

Athens, Ohio

two blue flowers
grew in my yard

in fact
they grew and retired
for several seasons
for vernal reasons

before I knew

they were in love

Athens, Ohio

Nuclear Family

resolving the actions of a nuclear family
requires the calling of kindred spirits
to the circle of Adamic fire
around which we gather our wits

refocusing the reactions of an unclear family
inspires the falling of hundreds of angels
from the mirth of higher planes
in which they usually flit

redefining old familial terms
defies the logic of genetic roots
and reboots the swollen feet
of ill computed logic

if we are to gather our forces
in combined familial energies
to move forward together
in carefully crafted synergies

whether we like the knots or not
the genealogical ties are the ones that bind
they bridge the synaptic gaps of illusion
leaving the fallow and inchoate behind

you can dabble in new clayic acid
and search with old alchemic means
but the thrust of who you are
and how you dream
is locked in relative obscurity

resolving the reactions of a nuclear family
requires the patience of heaps of generations
a silent dismembering of faces and places
around which we tether our saints
around which we gather our wits

Santa Fe

Window Dressing

the invasion ceases
       as the sun sets
and the lights go dim

streets which not long ago
thronged with hundreds
now bustle
       with only one

for the moment
just the broken man
       who droops to the corner
and stops
to peer reflectively
       in the dressed up window
       of a dress shop

he presses his hands
to the glass
   as if to ask
for a kiss
or plead for help
but then he bows his head
   to the elegance
that will never be his

and shuffles along his way
leaving behind that warm bed
   the chest full of drawers
   and things
and that female mannequin

with her outstretched arms

just a passing whim

Athens, Ohio

Splitting Heirs

ancient time fissures
      split the Akashic vellum
      into forgotten fragments
      that cavort in excitable rhythms
across modern time lines

they come as thoughts
unable to contain themselves
      in history books
      sitting forlornly and silently
      on the back shelves of eras
smiling impishly
      in our rear view bureau mirrors
modern time thoughts and happenings
impose on us the reality of now

future time visions
craft the present geography
      into edgy escarpments
      that cajole in impregnable patterns
beyond prehistoric land mines

they come as dreams
      unable to remain themselves
      in furtive looks
      hiding blithely like spirits
      in lost pages of epics

still laughing resoundingly
at our back door antics

Santa Fe

Chicago Intaglio
Commuter Train

screeching silver wheels
wedded to well-worn steel
a study of faces
races by
oh how quickly you could crush us

I, A Dancer

tendons stretching
elastic lasting
but
a musical cadenza

Grant Park

pools of pigeons
plankton gray and white
rippling on a velveteen tumble
of green grass

Airport

black reed
purple hat
an etching of a charcoal face
do your slender fingers
play your women
like they do your fine guitar

mondo cane
the world has gone to the dogs

an old brown mongrel
passed me on the street today
and said hello
which was rather strange
I would say

Athens, Ohio

imported from Ipswich
(to John Updike)

my little finger
seems an outcast
from the other
coordinated clique

Athens, Ohio

The Pittsburgh Boys

seems like a while back
often like a dream

those days when the steel mills screamed
        and the rivers lurched
under the weight of heavy laden barges
        on their way to somewhere
to build something big and strong and large

but there we were
the Pittsburgh boys
with funny names
        like Tree and Fido and Zero and Alley Cat
        and Corky and Porky
and Yablonski

making lots of noise

        dancin'
        prancin'
        romancin'
the girls the sports
        lost in the hills and the valleys
jumpin' the fences
        ridin' the trollies
crossin' the bridges

livin'
the long and short of growing up
in a together place
that always ran in pace
to a song
always to a song

we were the Pittsburgh boys
and still we are

wherever we are
on the roads we're on

     cool and strong

we'll keep going on

     because of where we're from

you remember that tune
it's all in that song you love
always in that song
     once in a blue moon
that's why
we're the Pittsburgh boys

Pittsburgh

colored dreams

i ache with pains
        of colored glass
        and rose window dreams
through which
i hear your face
        next to mine
        with
an inlaid emerald tear
an inlaid emerald tear

i ache with grains
        of sometime salt
        of different ways and means
through which
i see your voice
        next to mine
with an inlaid
kind of fear

Paris

Whirling pools

we are whirlpools
on the river of mind
vortices in the rock of sages
blossoms in the tree of winds

where ancient alluvial deposits
of the spheres
pebble our aspirations
with crumblings
from another lithosphere
washing onto the deltas
of our souls

we are but an iota of infinity

a bare quarter of a note
in the epic symphony of endless time

as we merge for a solitary moment
into the cleft of now

wherever that may be
we are whirling pools

Delray Beach

Circumference

my circles
are widening and flattening
floating
from hyperbola into parabola

circles circling
around a pi in the sky

seeking their distances
their spaces and their times
as we discover
and invent
or own geometry of human lines
and segments and arcs

and so it comes to this sharing
of circles
and the secrets
of their rhymes and quarks

who are you in time
and where in your circle
are you turning

you retrograde me
trying to reform my circle
into a box
for you to hide in

a circle takes no sides
a circle is a path

San Diego

Octagon

walked into an octagon
along a pointed path
strode upon a muted song
        a very loony tune

just to take a walk
along a new curve
rebirths a spirit line
without a set design

let it sing
let it sit
let it stir
        of frankincense and myrrh
of something gone along
        this way
a long time before

there's a message
in the muffled stones
where footprints gave them speech
untold songs and mystery notes
        and letters that they wrote

who needs them now
their syntax lost
the meanings smirched
the accents all but gone

came upon a stepped up pyramid
          fallow in its math
came upon a music space
          a rhythm on a merge

just to take a walk
behind an old nerve
revisions of an ancient time
without a clear design

let it spin
let it spit
let it reoccur
          of flesh and bone and fur
of something gone along
this way

a long time before

San Antonio

Space is the Place
Sun Ra

seeing again the rhythm of space
     in the hands of some
     who sculpt their place in the sands of tone
and rhythm bones

the providential almond tree
     sits against the paucity
     of arid lines in the sandy soil
or in the companionship
     of a stand of soul mates
     and their bovine friends
who gather round for respite
from the sun

where are the stones standing
in the plains above Salamanca
that angels left behind
are they hiding among the other brazen stones
or sheltering in some forgotten grotto
already hewn and taken for granite

Salamanca, Spain

Celtic Stoned
Salamanca, Spain

Celtic footprints
frozen
in igneous moments
of antiquity

why did they come here
those serial meanderers
the peripatetic sailors
the turned soil masters

to build in the stones
of other times and places
or to plant the cereal grains
of their own
across the plains

their crosses and stone circles
appear to harbor niches
far and wide
following stars and beams
of insight
long forgotten

set to atone

for transgressions
even more prehistoric
than their own

Beyond the Shadow of a Doubt

watching shadows dancing
on the white walls of the patio
energized by the settling sun

we are reminded
of our past entanglements
enhanced
      of course
      by beer and wine

as we balance
those fine lines
      of times gone by
with the temperaments of now

and just how
we still go forward
because the seeds of background
have long grown ahead of us

the sunrise of tomorrow
offers yet another glimpse
of friendships and kinships
sailing in the seas of here

these are the anchors of life
some harmony some strife
the tenets of how we all live
and fear and love

and like the dancing shadows
on the wall
this is how we all recall and rewind
those images dancing in the back of our minds

this is true

beyond the shadow of a doubt

Delray Beach

dream time

come take a walk with me
on the esplanade of my dreams
along the recourse of our schemes
    together and alone

come take a hike with me
right down the middle of this avenue
of speedy recognizance
    alone and together

let's go for a shift
right along the edge of recognition
meandering in that direction
    we can postpone
    or move along

we can fly off over there
through that rift in the shrouds
off to any time in somewhere
    like a drone or a feather

come take a ride with me
on this turtle's back
we'll take our time and talk a lot
but just about this and that

or we can just sit here on these rocks
deep in the mist of something
being a part or being a wedge
        depending on the tone and the meter

that's pretty much what you see
if you decide to take a walk with me
through the colonnade of dreamtime

suspending ourselves

from the tether
of our bones

Delray Beach

into the underbelly

down into the underbelly

        for a passing glance
        of what transpires in another space

that drifts along right beside us
        talking our language but in a twisted tongue
        making the words more angular and uneven
and hard to overstand

searching for some fragments of reality
        in tiny bits of truth that might embrace
        the chatter that blather around us
looking for shards of contentment
        that just might settle the dust of illusion
        that swirls around us

hunting down scraps of knowledge and fact
        guarded by a demon in the pit
        who bares its teeth at our approach

but we press along the way
believing that a stone unturned
        hides a glyph of sense
        perhaps within it

but finding only enigma and coded signs
we turn our attention back to faith
        in the intention of the ways we have learned
        from eras gone before
        reconceiving the most honest act of all

loving who we are
on our way back

        up

Delray Beach

All Hearts Vibe

all hearts vibe to the rhythms of life

imagine all the red together
        in a vessel of celebration
        sailing through the arteries of acceptance
        and exchange

all hearts vibe to the dances of time

        swaying to the lilt of pulse
        that beats a meter familiar to the feet
        of all souls who walk among us

all hearts bleed with the same losses

        of love and trial
        and pump us up with the same fortitude
        and never ending smiles

all hearts feel the throbs of endearment

       and adventure and fear of some unknown
       specter hiding secretly behind the thorns
       of lost love chances

all hearts vibe to the demands of time

       and the quickening pulse of emancipation
       and adoration
       plunging through the veins of silver linings
       that adorn the vast array of changes
       that breathe intention

deep into our souls

Delray Beach

The Tragedy of Sartoris Gibraltar

i stood rock still
the five o'clock multitude
multiplied
my embarrassment
for i knew
i was the banter of attraction
yet
i managed
with some nonchalance
to re-zip
my unzipped
zipper

Athens, Ohio

morning blooms

floral tongues

sticking from the windows

as dawn flowers yawn

and the city spills its children

onto the avenues

as bird breath clouds songs

among the blossoms

now lounging in morning review

Neuchatel, Suisse

For Brutus Was a Noble Son of a Bitch

he died a noble death
they said
and
he lived a good life
indeed
he was a fine man

a rotary man
an elk
went to the Y

saw him in church
beautiful kids
lovely wife

good job

a gentle happy man

everyone was so sad
when he died

but oh my god

if the others could have been there
when I saw this
happy man

crying in his bier

Athens, Ohio

Tatterdemalion
The Peanut Vendor

I moved toward him
with a tingle
of trepidation
and stared so long
at the white hairs on his face
and his tall black silk hat
and his long ebony fingers
and his pristine chalky teeth
and his tattered dark coat
and his mysterious primordial face

that I forgot about his peanuts

Athens, Ohio

hill sides

cow lines etch
bovine geography
pastoral calligraphy
and beast geometry
on the bucolic knolls
that amble linen covered
across soft green silk
on earthen thigh

the scouring hawk

the eye

minutely tucked inside
its coven
of soaring blue velvet

San Simeon, California

gateway

a workman with jack hammer
in hand

bounces the tawny brick town

to the admiration

of his small audience
standing at the gateway

wanting an audience
with the whispers
inside

Colombier, Suisse

falling

a leaf moves
with mouse inspired movements
into the woodpile

as a thought drifts
heavy
on the horizon

and

the day breaks
with new intention
draping colors
of pacific aspiration
along the foothills

as other fallen
leaves scatter
nervously

in search of a place

tucked safely away
from the dog
ways

Cambria, California

Dream Drinking

dark eye
peering
from a pillow peep hole
through the misty arras
of your hair
inking new lines
on the linen terrain
raining lightly
across your shoulders

waking
an awareness of awakeness
stretching and unstretching
like a sleepy spineless cat
we remove ourselves
from the tangled pattern
that we appliqued
during the night

knowing
that what passed for yesterday
is better left
dream drinking

Bloomington, Indiana

Samba Nova

just how did samba
get to be jive
and bossa
nova

Lisbon

naissance

being born
I built my house of wax
and
came Icariously close
to melting
into oblivion

Neuchatel, Suisse

ice capade

a sliver of arabesque ice
slides in a chilled amoebic moment
across the glassy hemisphere

playing an anxious game
of continental drift

between the rhythmic meter
of the windshield wipers

disappearing
at an imperceptible swish

into the tinted window sea

Chicago

do doo wop

the street corner guardian
an old but iron-willed mailbox
squats camouflaged
in the colors of the country
its rusty mouth agape
waiting to chew up the aspirations
of anyone who might think
an epistle is the easy way out

street corner colors fly
faintly yellow umber
and surely some blues
shining from the muted lights
prying into the night life
of a wandering sojourner

street corner sounds
a swirling urban harmony
a street corner prophet on his knee
an early morning hawker
a noon day fast talker
gesticulating with flair
an all day rocker
and a dog walker
adding to the hint of urine
in the air

street corner remnants
riding the crest
of a floating gaggle
of guttered refuse

      a hamburger wrapper
      a stone soul rapper
      a faded paper flower

a whiskey bottle
three times throttled
in the last hour
for its last drop

a forlorn condom yes
and...of course
the omnipresent shuffle
of a cop

street corner stone
on the corner stoned
holding up the day life
shining on the night life
shine on shine on

shaba doo wah
shaba doo wop

shaba doo wop
Cincinnati

Too Taboo

a sordid mom
assorted dads
a furtive look
a crooked groove

no matter what you say
no matter what you do
anywhere you go
someone's always yellin'
it's too too taboo

you're so inappropriate
what's the hope of it
what's the scope of it
you're too inappropriate

a forded stream
afforded schemes
a secret nook
a candid kind of look

no matter what you say
no matter how you pray
everywhere you go
somebody's always tellin' you
it's too too taboo

Santa Fe

97

Too Cool

What ever happened to cool

it just swaggered out of sight
drifted away
        into the dread of night
right on the back of Kerouac

What happened
to the slowness of momentum
        or the arc of understanding
to the fragrant beat of bop
the uniqueness of color
        and the pinpoint mostly of words

Where did cool go

the aura of presence
        on its vernacular tilt
the ghostly of words
        spoken with a lilt
the truth be told
the truth be bold
        without a hint of guilt

What happened to cool

to the essence of suede
that glint of gold
that aromatic jolt of leather
the reaction of feet to groove
the art of the show stopper
or dancing light as a feather

and damn...
now Dennis Hopper is dead!

What ever happened to being too cool

Taos

Everybody is Colored (a song)

everybody is colored
everybody's got tone
everybody's got a mother
and a bag of white bones

everybody is colored
everybody's got hue
no matter if it's me
no matter if it's you
everybody's got a mother
and a bag of white bones

the color of the night
the luster of gold
the color of fire
the swagger of bronze
everybody is colored just right

flax among gamboge
chromate tracks
in the saffron sand
flax among gamboge
everybody is colored
just right

everybody is colored
everybody's got shades
from the Queen of Hearts
to the Ace of Spades
everybody's got a mother
and a bag of white bones

everybody's got a mother
and a bag of white bones

Santa Fe

No Cafe in Burlington

there's no cafe in Burlington
no more

gone the way
of country life
just gone away

on the corner
used to be a cozy place
over there across the road

whole lotta town stopp'd by
at least once a week
usually in the mornin'
to chat and ruminate

she closed it
when her husband died
back awhile
just a while ago

come to think of it
'bout the same time
the whole town
just passed away

we're still mournin'
though no one cries now

she got a lil'ol coffee and donut place
down the end of that street
'bout a mile
no lunch and dinner though
just a lil'ol hole in the wall

only place to eat now
is up by the interstate
the way the crow flies

where everybody meets
now by accident
early in the mournin'

Burlington, Colorado

Alfama

an abundance of water
means a confluence of traveling cultures
and liquid tongues
Portuguese, Jewish and Moorish notions
somehow found this place
just across the oceans of time
gone by
now

the sanctity and security of this space
is everywhere tiled and glazed
and shared

everything

an arm's length embrace away
literally
face to face
as furtive eyes rather summarize
the welcome and the watchfulness
from just inside the open doorways
up the stairs
just around the corner

the feast of San Antonio
a tattered festoon away
water for the weary to drink
and to wash away
the stains that centuries leave behind
and
of course
the sins that glaze the guilt
along the twisted ways

as my glance tumbles down yet another
cobbled staircase
in my mind's eye

Alfama, Portugal

The Coimbra Poems
Coimbra, Portugal

Along the Coimbra Road

pine and eucalyptus
entangle
in a furry stand
of fragrance

Coimbra Universidad

the sounding of the bitch bell
a banshee cry
a peal of taunting domination
or
a musing of Minerva
maneuvering us to sainthood
in our little black cloaks
of scholarly attention
and detail

Monastic Life

Franciscan friars
and Santa Clara sisters
mingle in their monastic moments
signing covenants
and chanting breathless
words of love
in the towering convents of their minds
fathers, mothers
brothers and sisters
frolicking momentarily
as willful humans do
somewhere in the lower dominions
of their lofty aspirations
snug within the secret trysts
of earthly sanctity

The Porto Poems
Porto

perching anciently atop
an odd meandering confluence
of wine and convents
and hilly residential inclines
reclining royally
over misty mornings
and the antiquated moorings
that cultures left behind
punctuated by the raspy speak of sea gulls
calling and drifting in pools of attentive waiting
for an early morning fishing strike
she still perches there

Porto in the Fog

the fog is a stealthy visitor
cloaked in its own idiosyncratic mind
emphatic for a moment
then in a sudden other
gone with the wind

cruising up the Douro River
past an abandoned economy of silent hills
and rusted old machines
a former way of life
now roofless and left behind
with tiles and stones
the kindred that remain

gone with the escudo
but shielded still by wine
and protected by the providence
of valleys full of solitude

a new twist and turn
in the river of life
as tourists smile by

floating and unfolding
in the evolutionary mysteries
of time

Porto, Portugal

The Aromas of Sound

aromas and sounds abound in this place
some come with working
others with sleep
some come wafting
others sweeping into your senses
with the morning birds
the clacking trains and trolleys
that hustle time along
as bread bakes
and fish remains the aromatic
of everywhere

the tourist clatter
and camera clicks
the clack of shoes
along the cobbled stones
and walkways

the friendship of the pleasant pastries
can be inhaled from here
to Bethlehem

the sounds of bats
on the river
splashing through the ancient waterways
a rooster crows at the break of dawn
singing songs of stories
told along the ways

dogs bark at something
somewhere

rabelos glide through time
plying remnants of their wares
in modern casks of smiles

as the aromas rise
like old hearthen smoke
and sounds cavort
along the landscape
for many many miles

Douro, Portugal

Fado

roast pork potatoes soup and rice
and full frontal *fado*
for the soul
the darkly coiffed Katrina
singing with lyrical emotion
along the stringing sentiments
of love, hope and despair
and little to rejoice
but
let the muse entice
the beguiled traveler
to a hardy meal of faith
and little choice

deep in the tattered pockets of melody
and heartfelt musical motion

Bitetos, Portugal
Convento Alpendura

To Wallace Stevens

it was a New England morning
on a lonely barren beach
made sapphiric
by blue inflections
of the just now waking sun

when the clouds
were esoteric in the sky
and made meanderings of moments
and things
and ideas

when a camel
passed by

it was a camel
but soon it was a flower

a cluster in the rye

a *trompe d'oeil*

in the sky

a trick of the I

Boston

Freeing the me

it's come back to being me

a ragged circle
of tepid luminescence
a sudden pulse
of pygmy song
that tugs
at the omnipresent vapors
of indecision and insecurity

it's like the drive you used to take
as kids in the car
which my grandpa indignantly
called
the machine
the big black machine

are we there yet

let me now be bound
by the indigo of music
the blue of timelessness
to be cerulean free

it's come back to being me
owling at the moon
who, who are you
arcing at the dawn
a terra yawn

it's come back to being me
a ragged circle
of azure independence
and steamy mud

azure luminescence
and steamy mud

Santa Fe Summer Solstice

Winter Solstice Winter Light

at first light
on the dawn of a hoary
winter solstice morning
the sun spurts through
the kitchen window
sweeping down the hallway
into the laundry room

as the house revibes
into
megalithic Newgrange
Abrahamic Anasazi
the primordial slither
of Serpent Mound

a momentary gamboge dagger
pierces
into the heart of darkness
deep
into the soul of the laundry room

reminding me
with primitive raw
and a sultry
prismatic sense of awe

that the Promethean mysteries
of the universe
unfurl annually
for a mundane apollonian moment
to rekindle the infinite promise
of warmth
and winter light
and eternal rhythms

through my kitchen window

deep
into the soul of me
and my laundry room

Santa Fe

A New Seed (a song)

there's a new
seed in the wind
blowing around and about
looking for a place
to plant itself
and to grow

grow and grow

a full moon
throws it's light
across my path
a full moon
sheds it's skin
across my way

a multitude of animal
conversations
go on all around
in the background
some little chirps
some more profound

time is linen
hanging on the line
time is linen
flapping on the line

one end goes in
the other comes out
most of the time
it's just like that

we are messengers
tryin' to do our best
we are messengers
tryin' to fix this mess

changing spaces
irregular stones
changing faces
irregular tones

there's a new seed in the wind
blowing around and about
looking for some place
to plant itself
and to grow

grow and grow

a new seed

we are the roots of the new trees
of the many rooted banyan
we are the roots
and the arms and the knees

we are a new seed
bowing to the ground
befriending the rain fall
all around

in the back ground

a new seed

. **Santa Fe**

Coltrane

entanglements
in polka dots and moonbeams

engagements
round midnight
on parallel courses
it seems

and nocturnal admissions
lost arcs and frozen phrases
wholly wars of redemption
and tangled transgressions
play deeply

how deep is the ocean

lush lives
and moments of need
life with wings
and salt peanuts
swirl notably

bye-bye blackbird

these are a few

of our favorite things
Los Angeles

About the Author

Jack Kolkmeyer studied English Literature/ Creative Writing at Ohio University in the 1960's where he developed a special interest in the Romantic, Imagist and Beat poets. He was the Editor of *Sphere*, the Ohio University literary magazine, from 1967-68. His writings have appeared in numerous publications including *The Writers Place* and *The Liberian Literary Magazine* and have been broadcast on his popular Santa Fe radio programs, *The International House of Wax* and *Brave New World*, and presented with his performance group, The Word Quartet. Jack currently reads some of his work on his new radio project, Fifthwall Radio.

He was a Peace Corps Volunteer in Liberia, West Africa from 1969-72 and was greatly influenced by the emerging writers of that time, especially Leopold Senghor, Chinua Achebe and Amos Tutuola. Jack received an MPA in Public Policy/Urban and Regional Planning from Indiana University in 1974.

He moved to Santa Fe, New Mexico in 1975 to study filmmaking at The Anthropology Film Center and worked there professionally in education, broadcasting and the performing arts, journalism and urban and regional planning. Jack currently resides and writes in Delray Beach, Florida where his current writing projects include poetry, music and city planning topics, and screenplays.

A Philosophy of Yard is the author's second book, the first being *Higher Glyphics*.